Bible Sticker and Activity Book

Joseph's Coat of Many Colors

p

JOSEPH AND HIS BROTHERS

Long ago, in a land called Canaan, there lived a boy called Joseph. Joseph's father, Jacob, had many goats and many sons to look after them.

Jacob loved all his sons, but he loved Joseph best of all. Jacob gave Joseph a coat of many different colors. But this made Joseph's brothers angry and jealous.

Find the stickers of Joseph's eleven brothers to complete the picture.

Simeon

Judah

Reuben

Issachar

Gad

Dan

Asher

Levi

Benjamin

Zebulun

Naphtali

Using the numbers below, color in Joseph's colorful coat.

3

JOSEPH'S DREAM

One night, Joseph had a strange dream. The next day, he told his brothers about it.

"I dreamt that we were out in the fields, tying up bundles of grain," Joseph said. "When we were finished, your bundles made a circle around mine, and they all bowed down to it!"

Joseph's brothers grew even angrier with him.

"He thinks that we should all bow down to him!" they said.

Color in Joseph and his brothers.

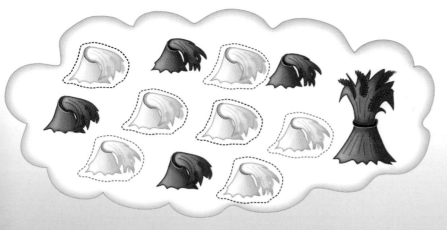

Find the stickers to finish the picture.
How many brothers does Joseph have? ☐
How many bundles of grain are bowing down? ☐

 Can you find eleven names hidden in this grid?

Simeon   Judah   Reuben   Issachar
Gad   Dan   Asher   Levi   Benjamin
Zebulun   Naphtali

```
S Z A W C G F V T G B
A B E N J A M I N D A
R Z E N U D B V E N S
Z E B A S I M E O N S
I B M P S E O L N B E
R U E H N H J Z M I L
E L V T Z L E V R J B
U U D A N S A R H U U
B N X L B N M J F D E
E W U I S S A C H A R
N J O L A V F C N H D
```

JOSEPH IN THE WELL

Joseph's brothers had had enough of him.

"Let's take his coat and kill him," said the brothers. But Reuben said, "No, let's throw him in the well and leave him there."

Find the stickers to finish the picture.

Later, some merchants passed by on their way to Egypt.

"Now we can get rid of Joseph!" Judah said. "We can sell him to the merchants as a slave."

The merchants bought Joseph for twenty pieces of silver.

The brothers decided to tell their father that a wild animal had killed Joseph. So they put goat's blood on Joseph's coat.

  Find the stickers to finish the picture.
Find the bag with twenty pieces of silver.
Follow the lines to find which merchant it belongs to.

JOSEPH IN PRISON

In Egypt, Joseph's master was a man called Potiphar.

Joseph worked hard for Potiphar, but Potiphar thought his wife was falling in love with Joseph, so he had him put in prison.

 Can you spot five differences between these two pictures?

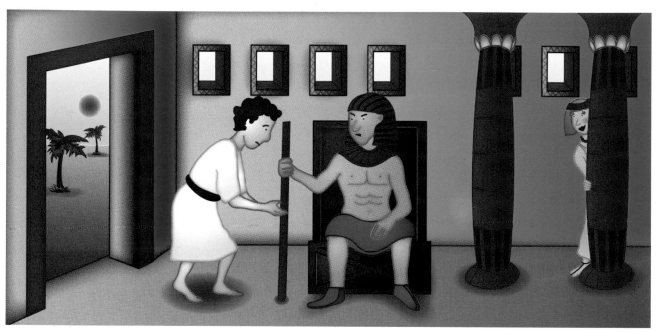

Page 2

Page 3

Page 5

Pages 6/7

Page 9

Pages 10/11

Pages 12/13

Page 14

One of the other prisoners was the butler of Pharaoh, the Egyptian King. One day, he told Joseph, "I had a strange dream last night. Can you tell me what it means?"

"God will tell us both," said Joseph. "What did you dream?"

"I dreamt I had a vine with three branches," said the butler, "and I made wine for Pharaoh."

"It means that in three days Pharaoh will set you free," Joseph told him.

Three days later, just as Joseph had said, Pharaoh set his butler free. The butler was amazed, and he told Pharaoh about Joseph.

  Find the stickers to finish the picture.
How many sets of three can you find in the picture?

PHARAOH'S DREAM

Some time later, Pharaoh had a dream that puzzled him. He remembered what his butler had told him about Joseph, and he asked for him to be brought from prison.

"I dreamed that I saw seven skinny cows eat seven fat cows," said Pharaoh. "Can you tell me what the dream means?"

"God can tell us both," said Joseph. "The dream means that Egypt will have seven years of plenty. But then there will be seven years of famine, when there will be very little food."

Find the stickers to finish the picture.

How many of each of these things can you find?

fans ☐   cats ☐   pots ☐   fat cows ☐   skinny cows ☐

THE BROTHERS' TEST

Pharaoh put Joseph in charge of Egypt's food stores. During seven years of plenty, Joseph saved the extra food. Then there was famine, but there was plenty of food for everyone in Egypt.

Back in Canaan, Joseph's family didn't have enough to eat. His brothers came to Egypt to buy grain. They didn't know that the person in charge was Joseph. But he recognized them.

He decided to test his brothers to see if they had changed. He filled all his brothers' sacks with grain. When no one was looking, he hid a silver cup in Benjamin's sack.

Find the stickers to finish the picture.

Find the stickers to finish the picture.
Which trail leads to Benjamin's sack?

a
b
c
d
e

FAMILY REUNION

When the cup was found in Benjamin's sack, the brothers were arrested and brought before Joseph.

Joseph said that the brothers could go home—except for Benjamin. Judah begged Joseph to let Benjamin go, too.

"We have already caused our father, Jacob, to lose one son," he said. "If he loses Benjamin too, he will die of sorrow."

Joseph saw that his brothers were sorry.

"I am your brother Joseph!" he cried. "Bring Father to Egypt, and we will be together again." So Jacob was reunited with his lost son, and the family lived together again.

 Find the story stickers and put them in the right order. Read the scrolls to help you.

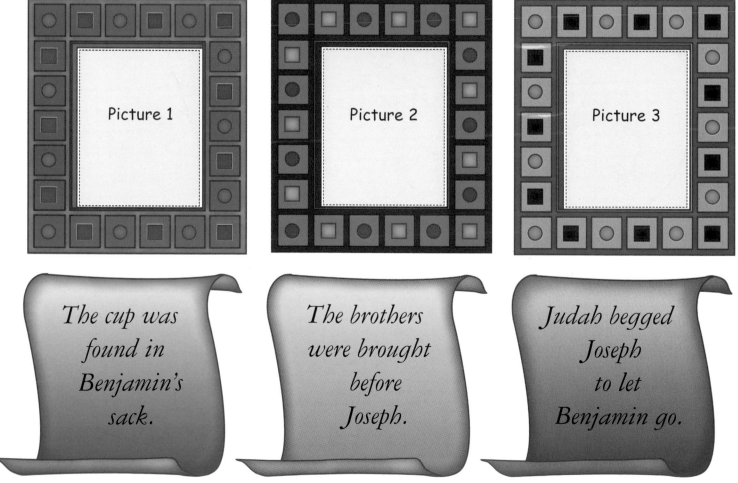

Picture 1

Picture 2

Picture 3

The cup was found in Benjamin's sack.

The brothers were brought before Joseph.

Judah begged Joseph to let Benjamin go.

Color in the picture of Joseph and Jacob's happy reunion. Can you find five mice hidden in the picture?

ANSWERS

Page 5

Page 7

Sack c contains
twenty pieces of silver.
It belongs to merchant c.

Page 8

Page 9

There are 7 sets of 3: 3 dream
stickers, 3 bars on the window,
3 seats, 3 bowls, 3 spoons,
3 prisoners (including Joseph) and
3 branches on the vine.

Pages 10/11

There are 7 fans, 7 cats, 7 pots,
7 fat cows and 7 skinny cows.

Page 13

Sack d belongs
to Benjamin.

Page 14

Picture 1   Picture 2   Picture 3

Page 15

S0-BCW-517

© PMI 1992

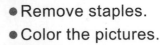
- Remove staples.
- Color the pictures.
- Add stickers to the blank spaces.
- Press out boxes and assemble as shown.

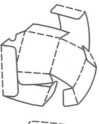

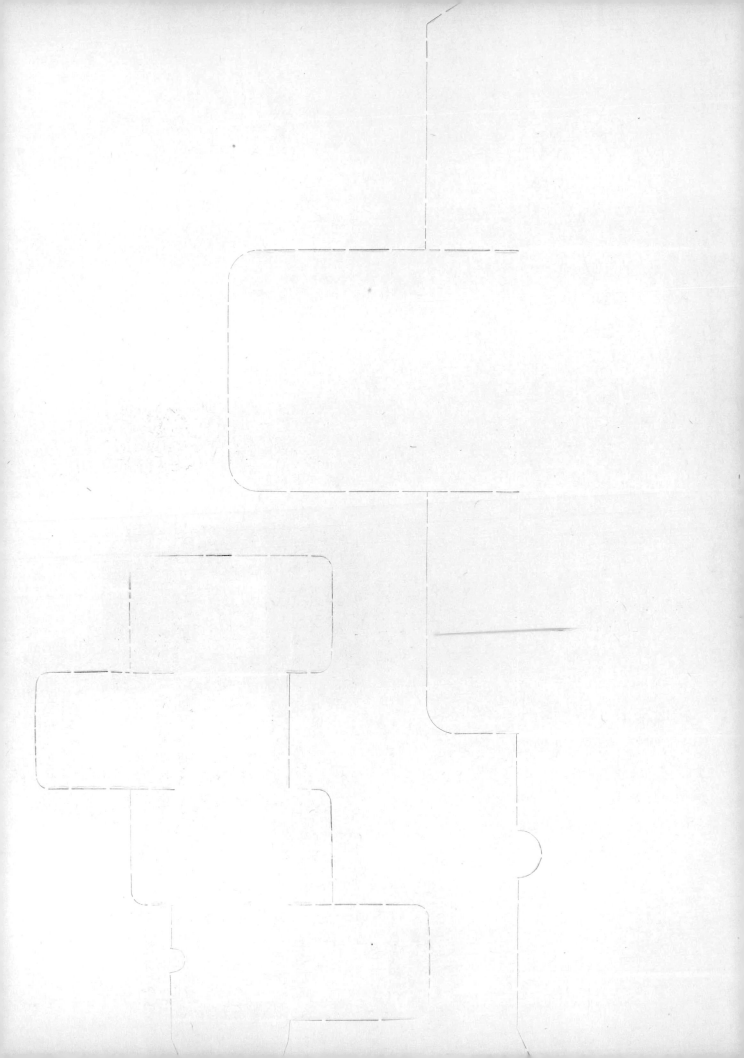

© PMI 1992